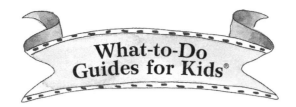
What-to-Do
Guides for Kids®

KT-199-748

What to Do When
BAD HABITS
TAKE HOLD

A Kid's Guide
to Overcoming
Nail Biting
and More

by Dawn Huebner, Ph.D.

illustrated by Bonnie Matthews

MAGINATION PRESS • WASHINGTON, D.C.
American Psychological Association

To my parents, Sondra and Gene Helfand, for helping to instill the good ones–DAH

What to Do When Bad Habits Take Hold is part of the Magination Press What-to-Do Guides for Kids® series, a registered trademark of the American Psychological Association.

Published by
MAGINATION PRESS
An Educational Publishing Foundation Book
American Psychological Association
750 First Street, NE
Washington, DC 20002

For more information about our books, including a complete catalog, please write to us, call 1-800-374-2721, or visit our website at www.maginationpress.com.

Library of Congress Cataloging-in-Publication Data

Huebner, Dawn.
What to do when bad habits take hold : a kid's guide to overcoming nail biting and more /
by Dawn Huebner ; illustrated by Bonnie Matthews.
    p.   cm. — (What-to-do guides for kids)
Summary: "Teaches school-age children cognitive-behavioral techniques for breaking habits such as nail biting and thumb sucking. Includes introduction for parents" —Provided by publisher.
ISBN-13: 978-1-4338-0383-3 (pbk. : alk. paper)
ISBN-10: 1-4338-0383-6 (pbk. : alk. paper)
1. Habit breaking—Juvenile literature.
I. Matthews, Bonnie, ill. II. Title. III. Series.
BF337.B74H84 2009
155.4'1233—dc22   2008017586

Manufactured in the United States of America
10 9 8 7 6 5

ECO-FRIENDLY BOOKS
Made in the USA

CONTENTS

Introduction to Parents and Caregivers

Stop biting your nails.

    Stop picking your nose.

      Stop picking your skin.

        Stop twirling your hair.

      Stop chewing your shirt.

    Stop pulling your eyelashes.

  Stop sucking your thumb.

It's exhausting, isn't it?

And the reality is, you can remind your child from now until the end of time. You can dangle rewards or threaten punishments. Use a calm voice. A stern voice. No voice at all. And it isn't going to make a bit of difference.

We all know it's almost impossible to simply stop a bad habit. Think about what it's like to *not* pop that extra cookie in your mouth. Not yell at your kids. Not clench your jaw. It takes determination that's sometimes hard to muster. Effort that's often hard to sustain. And even with effort and determination, it's just plain hard to do.

It's hard for adults, and it's hard for children, too—those little nail biters, shirt chewers, and thumb suckers who can't seem to stop their habit, regardless of their motivation to try.

But as you know, these sorts of habits can become problematic for kids. Their cuticles get bloody and sore. They get bald patches and chapped skin. Infected mosquito bites. Ingrown toenails. Snarled hair. And it doesn't end. Because in spite of the damage, in spite of the pain, they keep right on picking and pulling, rubbing and biting and chewing—until the motion itself becomes automatic. And by then the habit is locked in place. No wonder it's hard to stop.

That's why this book isn't about *stopping* bad habits. Willpower isn't mentioned, not even once (except right here). Instead, the focus is on breaking free from habits by dissolving the chains that keep them in place.

What to Do When Bad Habits Take Hold presents children with a set of strategies in the form of "keys" designed to unlock the chains holding habits in place. The methods are scientifically valid; the presentation is interesting, manageable, and fun.

While your child will be doing the bulk of the work, you, as parent or caregiver, can help. Read this book with your child, just one or two chapters at a time. Do all of the activities as directed; they will deepen your child's understanding and help with the shift from *knowing* to *doing*. The way to make this shift is clearly explained in the book, as is a reward system to help the process along.

Notice that you are rewarding your child's efforts to use what she is learning—not such things as how long her nails are or how smooth her skin might be. Consistent use of habit-busting strategies is the key to success and is more meaningful than nail growth, smooth hair, and the like, especially early on.

There is little evidence to suggest that the kinds of habits discussed in this book are indicative of deep-seated emotional problems. Kids who bite their nails, suck their thumbs, or twirl their hair are often no more stressed than their peers, although they do seem to need the physical sensations that come with their habits to regulate their internal state. Habits are calming for kids. And while they might be concerning to you, they don't necessarily mean that your child is struggling emotionally.

That's not to say that all children with bad habits are doing fine. Not all of them are. If you notice signs of stress—frequent worrying or perfectionism, meltdowns or trouble sleeping—it may be that your child does, in fact, need additional help. There are other titles in the **What-to-Do Guides for Kids®** series that can help your child learn to manage certain feelings and problems more effectively. But if there is

significant interference in your child's life, talk to your doctor to determine whether professional help is needed.

If your child is using a sharp implement or is otherwise engaging in a habit that frightens you, please seek medical assistance immediately. If the habit seems unusual to you—shrugging or throat clearing or grimacing—talk to your child's doctor to determine whether the habit might actually be a tic. Tics are common during childhood, and efforts to stop or change them are recommended only in specific circumstances. The methods described in this book are not the same as those used to treat tics.

But if your child has an ordinary habit such as nail biting, thumb sucking, hair twirling, scab picking, shirt chewing, nose picking, and the like, you are in the right place. The strategies presented in this book, when used over time, will help your child master something that has probably seemed impossible: breaking free from that pesky habit.

And your worn-out "stop it" refrain? You won't be needing that any more.

CHAPTER ONE

Getting Started

Remember way back, when you were a little baby? When you were just learning to walk? Just learning to talk? The world looked HUGE and sometimes scary. There were all sorts of things you couldn't possibly do, even if you really wanted to try.

You couldn't tie your own shoes.

You couldn't write your own name.

You couldn't even get a spoon to land in your mouth.

Those things were just too hard. It stayed that way for a long, long time.

climbing

reading

But then you started to learn. You learned to tie your shoes and write your name. You learned to eat correctly. You learned to walk and talk and add numbers together. You learned to snap your fingers and brush your teeth.

And everything you learned, even the things you can't really remember learning, you learned one step at a time.

Take washing your hands. Yup, even that was once tricky for you. There are lots of steps. You turn on the water. You squirt some soap, rub your hands together, and rinse them clean. It's easy now, and you go through all the steps without even thinking about them. But if you stand in a public bathroom, you'll hear parents holding their little kids up to the sink and telling them, "Rub your hands together." That's because little kids don't know they're supposed to do that.

But you know. You know because someone once taught you, and then you practiced over and over again. You practiced washing your hands so much that it became a habit.

A habit is something you do again and again, without really thinking about it.

Grabbing your backpack before you head out to school is a habit. So is reaching for your fork when you sit down to eat, or writing your name at the top of your paper. And even snuggling down in your favorite snuggle position before you fall asleep, that's a habit, too. You probably have a ton of habits. Everyone does.

Think of something you do in a certain way. Something you do again and again, without needing to think it through.

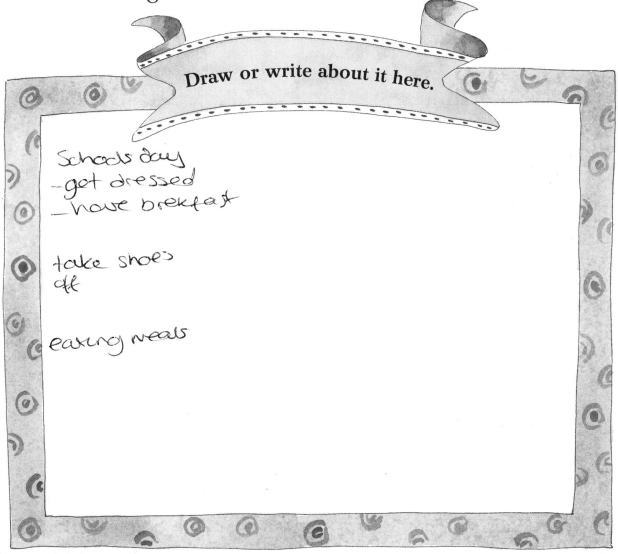

Draw or write about it here.

Schools day
—got dressed
—have brekfast

take shoes
off

eaking meals

People work at learning good habits. Your parents probably have some habits they want you to learn, things they remind you about now but want you to do on your own someday.

Put a check mark next to the helpful habits you already have and the ones you're working on learning.

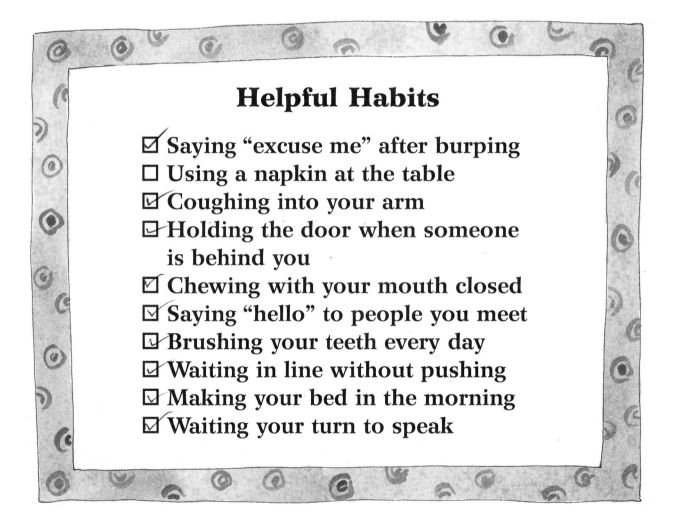

Helpful Habits

☑ Saying "excuse me" after burping
☐ Using a napkin at the table
☑ Coughing into your arm
☑ Holding the door when someone is behind you
☑ Chewing with your mouth closed
☑ Saying "hello" to people you meet
☑ Brushing your teeth every day
☑ Waiting in line without pushing
☑ Making your bed in the morning
☑ Waiting your turn to speak

These are all helpful habits. Helpful habits are polite. Or they keep you healthy, or make your day run more smoothly. Helpful habits are habits to hold on to.

But there are other kinds of habits, too. Habits that aren't healthy. Habits that end up causing PROBLEMS for people. Most of us have a few of these not-so-helpful habits.

Think about all the people you know: grown-ups, kids, even yourself. Put a check mark next to each not-so-helpful habit if you know at least one person who does it.

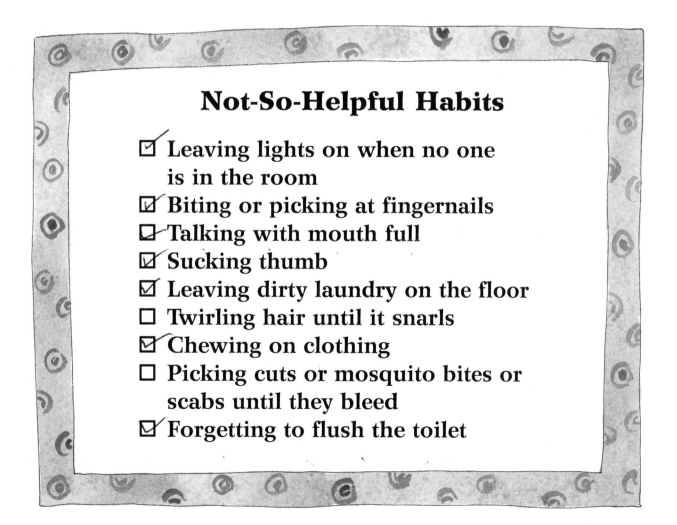

Not-So-Helpful Habits

☑ Leaving lights on when no one is in the room
☑ Biting or picking at fingernails
☑ Talking with mouth full
☑ Sucking thumb
☑ Leaving dirty laundry on the floor
☐ Twirling hair until it snarls
☑ Chewing on clothing
☐ Picking cuts or mosquito bites or scabs until they bleed
☑ Forgetting to flush the toilet

If you're reading this book, chances are good that you have a not-so-helpful habit.

Congratulations! Not because you have bad habits, but because you're admitting to them. Some people try to pretend that their bad habit isn't a bad habit at all, which is pretty ridiculous when you think about it.

And some people feel ashamed about their bad habits, maybe because those habits have been the focus of so much negative attention.

You have probably tried to stop your bad habit. Maybe lots of times. Well, guess what? You don't have to do that anymore.

That's right. From now on, you don't have to try to *not* suck your thumb or *not* bite your nails. You don't have to work on stopping whatever it is you're doing. That's because it's nearly impossible to simply STOP a bad habit.

But it is possible, very, very possible, to develop a new habit, and to make the new habit take the place of the old habit, so that the old habit doesn't bother you anymore.

Lots of kids have learned to do it. And you can, too. Keep reading and you will learn how.

Locked Up Tight

Long ago, your habit wasn't a habit. It was something you did, just once.

There was a first time you stuck your thumb in your mouth. Or pulled out a hair. Or chewed on your shirt or bit off a fingernail. And that very first time, whatever you did accomplished something for you.

The first time you nibbled on a fingernail, you were probably trying to even out a rough spot.

The first time you yanked out a hair, you might have been trying to get rid of one that was thicker than the others, or shorter, or kinkier. Or maybe you were bored and started playing with your hair, and pulling one out gave you something to do.

Body habits start when you need to accomplish something. You need to fix something or soothe something or get something done.

Take nose picking. If you're a nose picker, you have discovered that using your finger is a handy way to clear out the crusty or gooky stuff that gets stuck in your nose. You reach your finger in, pick out whatever is there (or just explore to see if anything is there), and then it feels better.

It works that way with any body habit—nail biting and thumb sucking and all the rest. All body habits get some sort of job done, which is one of the reasons why they're so hard to stop. If you didn't pick your nose, how would you get rid of the gunk? If you didn't bite your fingernails, how would you smooth out the jagged edges?

That's where new habits come in. The best way to get rid of an old habit is to find something new that gets the same job done, and then practice doing the new thing instead.

Blowing your nose, for example, is another way to clear out the gunk. It's a little more complicated than using your finger, so you'll need to practice, but it works just as well. And if you do it over and over again, nose blowing will eventually replace nose picking. VOILA—a new habit!

HONK!

It's the same with nail biting. And thumb sucking. And hair twirling. And shirt chewing. And skin picking. And just about any body habit you can think of. You can replace old habits with new ones.

Okay, you're right, it's a bit more complicated than that. It takes more than keeping a box of tissues nearby to form a new habit, and more than deciding to blow your nose to actually stop the picking.

That's because, as it turns out, there are lots of things that habits accomplish for you. Even bad habits.

Let's stick with nose picking. Nose picking does more than just clean out your nose. It keeps your hands busy. It briefly soothes your sore spots. It may even help you concentrate. So nose picking actually helps you in lots of ways. It's the same with hair twirling and shirt chewing and all the rest.

You might be wondering if this book is going to help with your habit, because nail biting is different from shirt chewing, which is different from thumb sucking, which is different from scab picking, and so on. So how can one book possibly help?

One book can help because all body habits—*all* of them—help kids in the same ways. But then they get LOCKED in place. And even if you want to break free, you can't.

Unless, of course, you have the keys.

Because whatever your particular habit is, the chains that hold it in place can be opened with a set of keys. Five keys, actually. And whether your habit is nail biting or thumb sucking or shirt chewing or hair twirling or any other body habit, these same five keys will set you free.

Key #1: Getting in the Way

You have a name. So does everyone you know. Hamsters have names. Dogs and cats and horses, too. Streets have names, and states and countries. Television shows. Songs. Fancy sandwiches in restaurants. And keys. That's right, keys have names (at least the ones in this book do). It's your job to find out what they are.

Solve this riddle to find the name of your first key. When you think you know it, turn the page.

The key that comes first

Ends with an "ock,"

Making it rhyme

With sock, flock, and clock.

It's made out of wood,

Or plastic, or rock.

The key that comes first,

You now know is

— — — — —.

Your first key is the **BLOCK** key.

There are two meanings for the word "block." One is the kind of block you build with. The other means to get in the way or stop something from happening.

The police block off a street before a parade so cars can't get through.

A really tall person might block your view at the movie theater.

And you are going to learn to block your habit, because that's what this key is about.

Blocking a habit means doing something that gets in the habit's way. Blocking helps you notice what you're doing, so you can switch to something else instead.

You can block nail biting by putting bandaids over your nails, or thumb sucking by wearing lightweight gloves to bed. You can block eyelash pulling by putting petroleum jelly on your eyelashes (it makes them hard to grasp), or mosquito-bite picking by keeping your bites covered.

You have probably noticed that the part of your body used during your habit feels DIFFERENT from the area around it. It's calloused, or prickly, or sore. You may be surprised to know that this difference is part of what keeps your habit going. You're drawn to this odd-feeling place. You want to touch it with your hands, or place it in your mouth. It hurts and needs soothing, or it's interesting and needs to be explored. Before you know it, you're doing your habit again.

But when you use the block key to get in the way of your habit, your nails or hair will start to grow. Your skin will start to heal. The rough and prickly and sore parts of your body will begin to smooth out. And you won't be so attracted to them, because they will feel just like the rest of your body.

The block key is an important first step toward getting rid of your habit. So let's figure out how to make it work for you.

🔒 Write the name of your habit on the top line of the empty box.

🔒 List the parts of your body and the objects you use to do your habit.

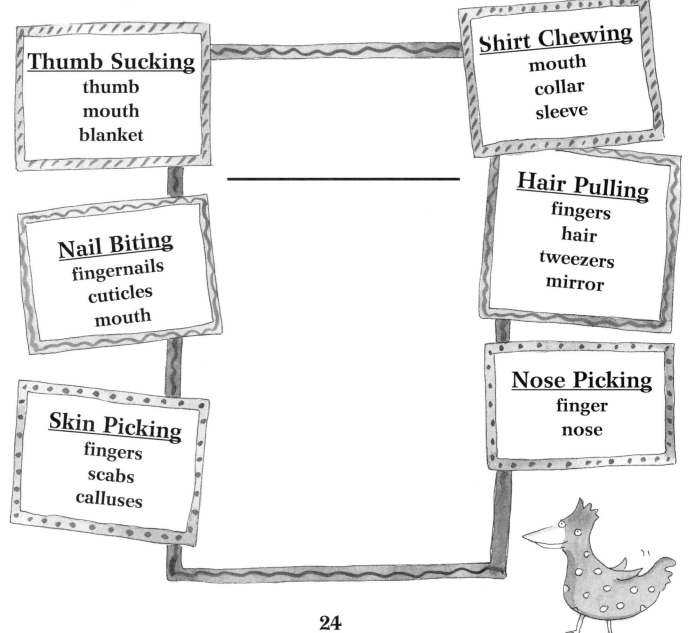

Thumb Sucking
thumb
mouth
blanket

Shirt Chewing
mouth
collar
sleeve

Nail Biting
fingernails
cuticles
mouth

Hair Pulling
fingers
hair
tweezers
mirror

Skin Picking
fingers
scabs
calluses

Nose Picking
finger
nose

Take a look at the list you just made. Can you think of a way to block your habit by covering or changing one of the things you use?

Let's say your habit is rubbing and picking the flat part of your thumbnail. The habit involves your thumbnail and the nail on your middle finger (the one you use to do your picking). Here's what your block plan might look like:

Block Plan

1. **Put a bandaid over my thumb.**

2. **Wear a glove to bed.**

3. **Wrap the top of my thumb with gauze.**

4. **Put a latex tip over my thumb.**

5. **Put a bandaid over my picking fingernail.**

Or maybe your habit is pulling hair from the back of your head. You use your hair, your fingers, and sometimes tweezers to do it.

Block Plan

1. Wear a hat or bandanna, even at night.

2. Keep my hair pulled back in braids or pony tails.

3. Put bandaids around my pulling fingers (thumb and pointer).

4. Wear latex fingertips.

5. Put lotion on my fingers and conditioner in my hair, so it's too slippery to pull.

6. Have my mom or dad hide the tweezers.

Sometimes the most obvious way to block a habit isn't very practical, especially when the habit involves your mouth.

Don't let that stop you. Block the habit by covering your fingernails so you can't bite them, or by choosing shirts with non-stretchy collars so you can't suck them. Be creative. There's always something you can do to get in the way of your habit.

Write your block plan here.

Block Plan

1._____

2._____

3._____

4._____

5._____

6._____

🔒 Flip to page 71 at the back of the book, where it says Habit-Busting Keys. Find the first key and label it the BLOCK key.

🔒 On the lines next to the key, fill in your block plan.

Now you have the first of your five keys. Start using it right away.

And remember...

Someone tall might block your view.

Shades block sun from shining through.

A clothespin's great to block the "pew."

And you can BLOCK your habit, too!

POOF

Key #2: Busy, Busy

One of the useful things about habits is that they keep your hands, and sometimes your mouth, busy. Busy-ness is what this next key is about.

Solve this puzzle to find the name of your second key. (Hint: Write the first letter of each word on the line above the picture.) When you have all the lines filled in, turn the page.

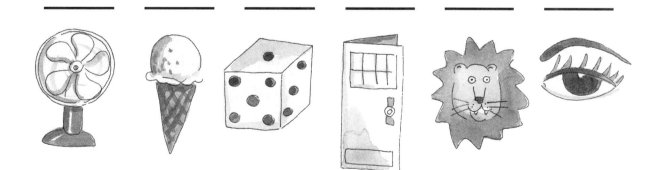

Your second key is the **FIDDLE** key.

Many kids have hands (and mouths) that need to move. A lot. Hands that need to touch and squeeze and pick at things. Mouths that need to nibble and suck and chew. It's nothing to be ashamed of, and there's no need to be angry at your hands or your mouth. It's not their fault, either! That's just the way it is for some kids.

But instead of doing things that lead to painful cuticles, or crooked teeth, or wet spots on your shirt,

 and instead of picking your mosquito bites into major sores, or twisting your hair into major knots,

and definitely instead of saying NO NO NO to your hands and your mouth (which we all know doesn't work), you need to keep busy in some other way.

That's where the fiddle key comes in.

There are countless ways to fiddle—to keep your hands and mouth busy. The key is to find things that are interesting and fun. Like eating watermelon. That keeps your hands busy. Your mouth, too.

But you can't exactly snack on watermelon during a spelling test. Or in the car. Or at church. And you wouldn't want to eat all the time, anyway.

So the trick is to find things you can do all the time, or at least as often as you need to. And in all the right places. During spelling tests. In the car. Even at church.

ake the fiddle key work for you, think about the places you tend to do your habit, and the things you do when you're in these places. These are called your **DANGER** zones. Here's what your list might look like:

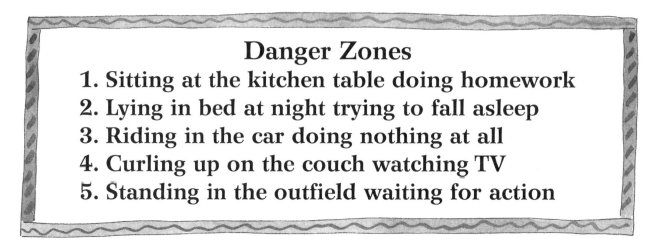

Danger Zones
1. Sitting at the kitchen table doing homework
2. Lying in bed at night trying to fall asleep
3. Riding in the car doing nothing at all
4. Curling up on the couch watching TV
5. Standing in the outfield waiting for action

Write your list of danger zones on the numbered lines below. (You'll add fiddle ideas in a minute.)

Danger Zones   **Fiddle Ideas**

1._____   ☐ ☐

2._____   ☐ ☐

3._____   ☐ ☐

4._____   ☐ ☐

5._____   ☐ ☐

6._____   ☐ ☐

Look at the following lists of fiddle ideas, or use your own imagination to think of ways to keep your hands or mouth busy in each of your danger zones.

To Keep Hands Busy

Play with a koosh ball

Play with silly putty or clay

Doodle

Toss a ball from
hand to hand

Knit

Rub a smooth stone
or a strand of beads

Tie knots in a piece
of string

Pet a dog or cat

To Keep Mouth Busy

Chew gum

Suck hard candy

Chew a thin straw

Nibble a piece of
raw spaghetti

Play an instrument

Practice whistling

Floss teeth

Sing

Count teeth
with tongue

Curl tongue
from side to side

Write your favorite fiddle ideas in the empty boxes next to each of your danger zones on page 32. Add your own ideas, too. Be creative.

Gather the materials you need for your fiddle activities, and put them in your danger zones. A stress ball and silly putty by the TV. Straws in your backpack. A CD to sing along with in the car. Make sure you have the items you need in the places you need them most.

Grab a fiddle tool as soon as you enter a danger zone.

If you chew on your shirt while doing homework, pop a piece of gum in your mouth *before* you open your science book. If you pick your scabs in the car, pull out a spare shoelace and challenge yourself to tie 40 knots the instant your seat belt clicks shut.

Don't wait until you're actually doing your habit to start fiddling. By then it will be too late. Use your fiddle activities before your habit has a chance to kick in.

🔒 Turn to your Habit-Busting Keys on page 71, and label your second key FIDDLE.

🔒 Write your fiddle activities on the lines next to the key.

Start using the fiddle key right away to keep your hands (or mouth) happily occupied.

Know your ___ ___ ___ ___ ___ ___

___ ___ ___ ___ ___•

Keep your hands or mouth ___ ___ ___ ___

when you are in these zones.

Use your fiddle tools ___ ___ ___ ___ ___ ___

you actually need them.

CHAPTER FIVE

Key #3: Pick, Pull, and Chew

Sucking and picking and twirling. Biting and pulling and chewing. Your hands and your mouth really want to be doing these things. It's almost as if they have a mind of their own. That's why you need this third key.

Solve the riddle to find the name of the key. When you think you know the answer, turn the page.

Your third key:

BOING BOING

Rhymes with ocean,

Is spelled like potion,

Soothes you, like lotion,

Can cause a commotion,

Do you have a notion?

You guessed it,

It's __ __ __ __ __ __!

PSSST! IT'S ANOTHER WORD FOR 'MOVEMENT'.

Your third key is the **MOTION** key.

You may have noticed that body habits all start with action words.

You **BITE** your fingernails or **TEAR** your toenails, **CHEW** your cuticles or **SUCK** your thumb. You **LICK** your lips or **PICK** your scabs or **SCRATCH** a certain spot on your hand, over and over again.

🔒 Circle the action word that best describes your habit.

Homework for
TUESDAY

1. Paper bag project
2. Math worksheet
3. Action word sentences

Action Words

Bite   Pick   Scratch
Tear   Pull   Twirl
Chew   Lick   Rub
Suck   Yank   Nibble

Ms. Arnold - Room 204   BEST TEACHER

The word you circled is the motion that goes with your habit. It's what you do with your hands or your mouth. Other people might not understand this, but that motion feels good to you. It settles you down or relieves you in some way.

And yet it's hurtful, too, leaving sore spots that never quite heal. So the trick is to find a way to do that same motion without hurting yourself. To find something else to bite or yank or scratch or chew. Something other than your own body.

Here's how it works:

If you SUCK your thumb, you could:

Suck a candy cane

Suck applesauce through a straw

Suck a clean, damp cloth

Suck water through a sip cup

If you TEAR your nails with your teeth, you could:

Tear strands of string cheese

Tear shreds of dried pineapple

Tear strips of beef jerky

If you PULL your hairs, you could:

Pull weeds from the garden

Pull fuzz from wool blankets

Pull hair from old dolls

Pull feathers from a duster

If you PICK your skin or scabs, you could:

Pick stickers from boxes

Pick pieces off an old foam ball

Pick fuzz from fleece sweatshirts

Pick nail polish from plastic

As you're thinking about your habit's motion, get a clean washcloth that your parents can spare. Pick at the washcloth, or rub it, or suck it. Whatever your habit's motion is, do it to the washcloth. Then think about what else you could use in place of the washcloth—and instead of your body. What would be the right firmness or softness or wetness? What would feel good to pick or rub or chew?

Write your ideas here.

🔒 Turn to your Habit-Busting Keys on page 71, and label the third key MOTION.

🔒 Write your three favorite motion ideas on the lines next to the key.

Start using the motion key right away. Aim for twice a day (more is even better). You can use the motion key whenever you get the urge to do your habit. Or schedule it in shortly before entering one of your danger zones.

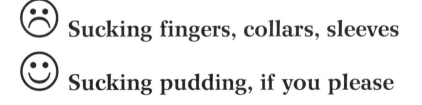

Nibbling nails down to the nub

Nibbling noodles, seeds, a sub

Sucking fingers, collars, sleeves

Sucking pudding, if you please

Twirling hair, a messy tangle

Twirling string, a playful dangle

Key #4: Perk! Jazz! Zing!

Why does one person become a nail biter, while another becomes a hair puller? Or a skin picker? Or a lip licker? Habits like these develop when one part of your body needs extra ATTENTION.

That's what this fourth key is about. Solve the puzzle to find its name. (Hint: transfer the letters from the boxes to the lines above. Don't use the letters that are crossed out.) When you think you know the answer, turn the page.

Your fourth key is the **WAKE-UP** key.

The wake-up key gives your body a workout, **PERKING** or **JAZZING** or **ZINGING** the areas that need to get some extra attention.

How does it work? Let's say you have a mouth habit, like thumb sucking or shirt chewing. That means it's your mouth that needs extra attention, some jazzing up to make it happy. So during one of your regular meals, instead of the same boring foods you usually eat, try:

Different Textures

Bumpy:
    seeds, whole-wheat
    crackers
Crunchy:
    celery, peppers
Juicy:
    watermelon,
    plums

Different Flavors

Sour:
    green apples,
    lemons
Salty:
    pretzels
Strong:
    juice concentrate,
    pickles

Different Motions

Chewing:
    raisins, gum
Sucking:
    yogurt through
    a sip cup
Slurping:
    spaghetti
    strand by
    strand

And if it isn't a mealtime, you can still keep your mouth in motion:

Chewing on straws or rubber toys

Gargling with mouthwash or salty water

Running your tongue over your teeth, around and around

RUBBER TOYS

GARGLING

PLUMS

RUNNING TONGUE OVER TEETH

RUBBER DUCKY

CHEWING GUM

GUM

RAISINS

STRAWS

CRACKERS

LEMON

If it's your scalp that needs extra attention, you can:

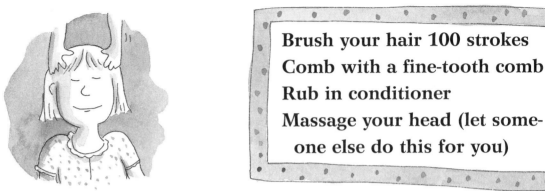

Brush your hair 100 strokes
Comb with a fine-tooth comb
Rub in conditioner
Massage your head (let some-
one else do this for you)

If your fingertips or fingernails need some action, you can:

Use an emery board to file
your nails
Rub lotion onto your nails
and cuticles
Put together a box of textured
items to touch and play with

ZIPPER BEADS SCRUBBY

If your skin needs perking, you can:

Use a massager
Have someone lightly scratch or tickle you
Have someone wrap you tightly in a blanket
so your skin and muscles feel the squeeze
Roll down a grassy hill, wearing shorts
Rub large areas of your skin with different
materials, such as a towel, a silky scarf,
a fleece blanket, some corduroy

Shade or draw the parts of your body that you use for your habit.

What are three things you can do to wake up these parts of your body?

Things I Can Do to Perk! Jazz! Zing!

1. _____

2. _____

3. _____

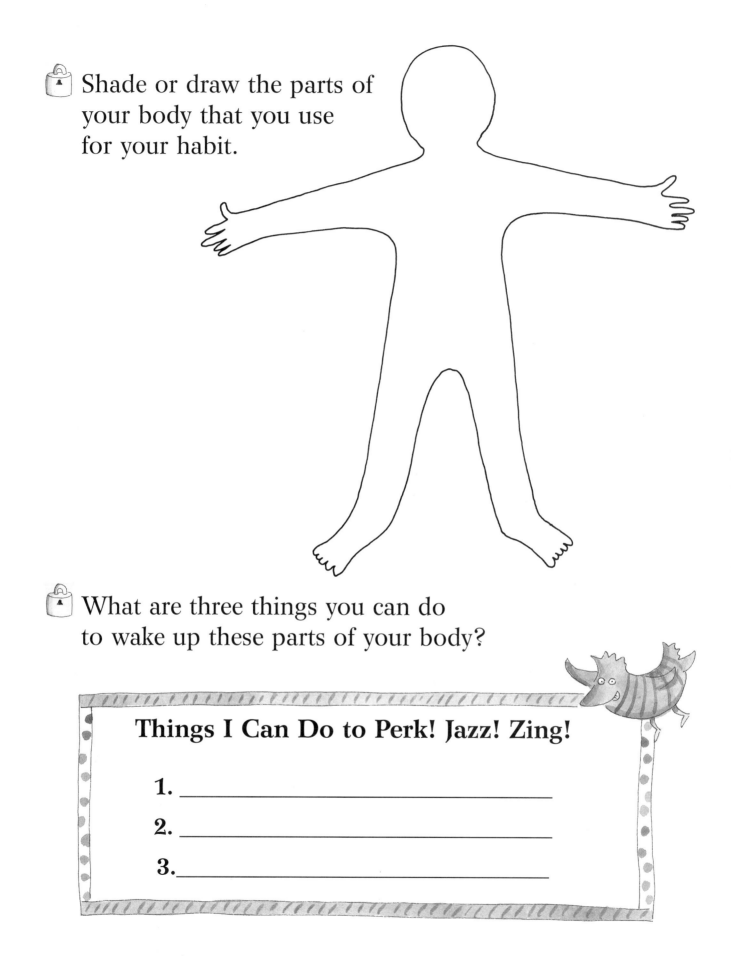

47

The wake-up key needs to be used at least twice a day, whether or not you feel the need for it. Most kids find it helpful to actually schedule time for this key, once early in the day and once later in the day. More often is fine, too.

 Turn to your Habit-Busting Keys on page 71, and write WAKE UP on the fourth key.

Write your three favorite wake-up ideas on the lincs ncxt to thc kcy.

Start using your wake-up key today. The perking, jazzing, and zinging will feel good, and another chain will fall away.

And remember...

(Hint: transfer the letters from the boxes to the lines above, and don't use letters that are crossed out.)

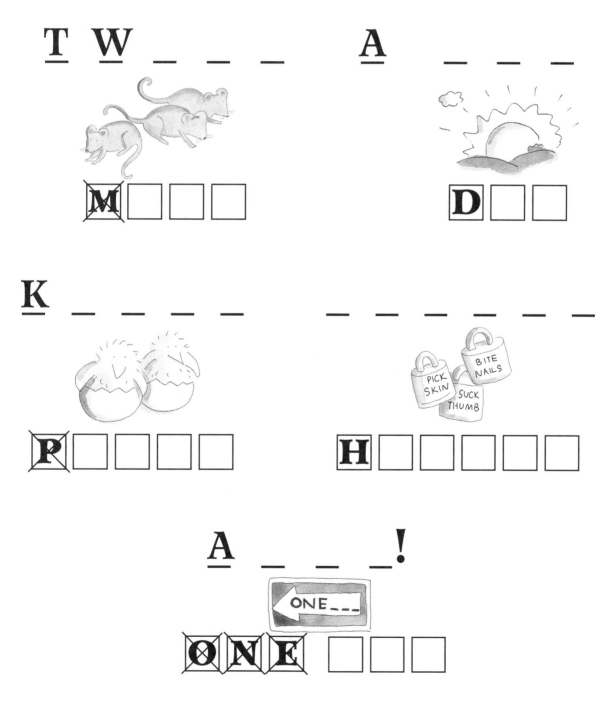

T W _ _ _   A _ _ _

~~M~~ ☐ ☐ ☐   D ☐ ☐

K _ _ _ _ _

~~P~~ ☐ ☐ ☐ ☐   H ☐ ☐ ☐ ☐ ☐

A _ _ _ _ !

~~O~~ ~~N~~ ~~E~~ ☐ ☐ ☐

Key #5:
Draining Tension

People assume that kids with body habits are anxious. In fact, you may have heard nail biting, skin picking, and such called NERVOUS habits. But not all kids who bite and twirl, pick and pull, rub and chew are nervous. Some are bored instead. Or frustrated. Or excited or sad or confused.

That's where this next key comes in.

Match each face with the emotion word that describes it. Then write the first letter of the word on the line above the face. When you think you've solved the puzzle, turn the page.

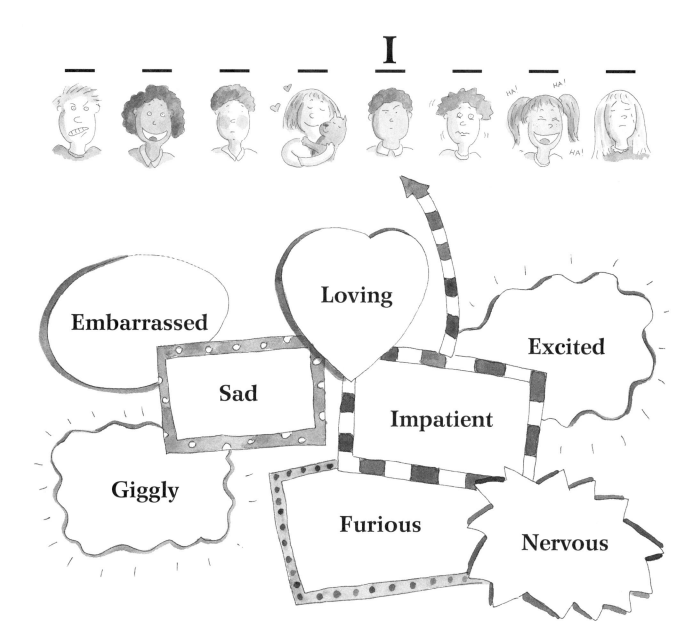

I

Embarrassed

Loving

Excited

Sad

Impatient

Giggly

Furious

Nervous

The fifth (and final) key is the **FEELINGS** key.

We all feel things, pretty much all the time. Sometimes our feelings are small, and we hardly notice them. Kind of happy. A little bored.

But other times, our feelings are big. ANGRY. GIGGLY. EMBARRASSED. When our feelings are big, they take up lots of space.

It's like a balloon filling with air. Lots of air fits in. But if the air keeps filling the balloon, the balloon will eventually burst.

People are like that, too. We can hold lots of feelings, but sometimes it gets to be too much.

In the case of a too-full balloon, the solution is simple. Open the mouth of the balloon and let out the extra air.

With people, it isn't quite that easy. For one thing, it isn't air that needs to be let out. It's TENSION. Tension is what builds up in our bodies when we feel certain feelings. A little tension is a good thing. It helps us feel energetic and lively. But too much tension doesn't feel good. It needs to be released.

There are lots of ways to release tension. Laughing and crying and talking and singing and running around all drain tension from our bodies.

Habits drain off tension, too. In fact, once a habit is locked in place, it becomes a quick and easy way to shrink our feelings down to size.

Sometimes, the way that habits relieve tension is obvious. Sucking, for example, is soothing to most people. There's a rhythm to it that feels comforting. It's the same with rubbing and twirling.

But what about habits that hurt? Is there really something soothing about tearing a cuticle or yanking out a hair?

Actually, there is. Not during the tearing or yanking, but afterward. These kinds of habits create a quick, sharp pain that for many kids is followed by a feeling of relief. The sharp pain releases tension, and the relief that comes afterward locks the habit in place.

So if you have one of these habits, do you need to keep hurting yourself to get rid of tension?

No, you definitely don't need to do that. Plenty of other things can help. That's why you have a feelings key.

Here's a list of activities that go along with the feelings key. All of them relieve pressure, shrinking big feelings down to a manageable size.

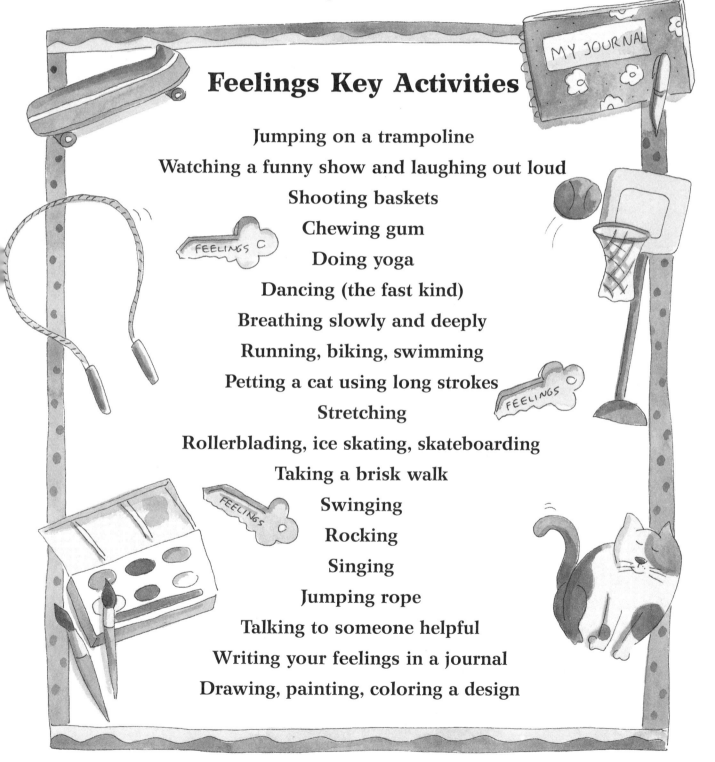

Feelings Key Activities

Jumping on a trampoline

Watching a funny show and laughing out loud

Shooting baskets

Chewing gum

Doing yoga

Dancing (the fast kind)

Breathing slowly and deeply

Running, biking, swimming

Petting a cat using long strokes

Stretching

Rollerblading, ice skating, skateboarding

Taking a brisk walk

Swinging

Rocking

Singing

Jumping rope

Talking to someone helpful

Writing your feelings in a journal

Drawing, painting, coloring a design

Fifteen minutes with a feelings key activity is all you need to drain off that extra tension, so you won't need your habit to do it for you.

 Turn to your Habit-Busting Keys on page 71, and label the fifth key FEELINGS.

 Write down your three favorite tension drainers.

It's especially helpful if you use your feelings key before entering a danger zone. Go for a bike ride before settling down for homework. Pump high on your swings before getting into the car.

You can also use the feelings key when you're feeling something big, especially if there is no one nearby to talk to. Try petting your cat when you feel sad. Do yoga when you're confused. Shoot baskets when you're angry.

While tension drainers won't solve your problems, they can help turn big feelings into much smaller ones so you won't need to nibble your nails or pick at your skin to feel better inside.

Pay attention to your

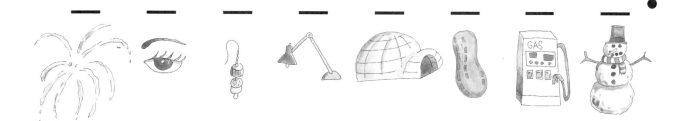

Drain them when they get too

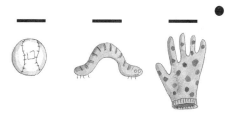

Putting It All Together

Now you have all five keys. Your key ring is complete.

Of course, keys don't do anyone any good if they're left lying around. You have to actually use them. And in the case of habit-busting keys, you have to use them over and over again.

Well, scientists have discovered that it takes 21 days to change a habit. That's three weeks. Three weeks of using all five keys. Every day. Practice is a really important part of getting your keys to work.

But sometimes it's **HARD** to practice.

That's where rewards come in. Rewards give you something to look forward to. A reason to keep working, even when the work is hard. Rewards help you use your keys long enough to break free.

So what would be fun for you?

Maybe you want to earn a restaurant breakfast with your dad. Or a miniature golf date with your mom. You could bake cookies with a friend. Get a manicure. Watch TV on a night when you're usually not allowed.

Be creative. Think of four rewards that would help motivate you to practice using all of your keys.

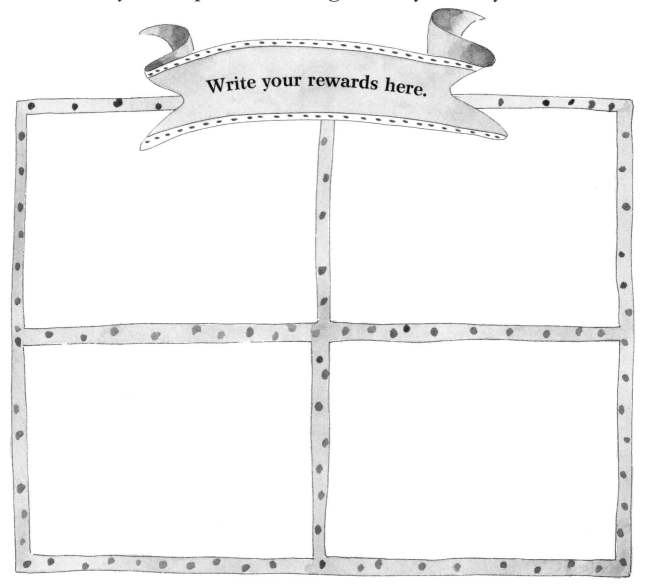

Write your rewards here.

So how do you earn these great rewards?

Take a look at the Breaking Free chart on page 72, the very last page of this book.

Each day, record the date on the chart. Then color the keys you use that day. If you use one key, you get one point. If you use four keys, you get four points. One point per key per day. As soon as you have 30 points, you get a reward.

If you keep forgetting certain keys, think of a plan to help you remember. Put the bandaids right next to your bed. Keep a jar filled with gum on the table where you do your homework. Slap up a sticky note in the car.

The fastest way to break free from your habit is to use all five keys every day. It just so happens that that's the fastest way to earn rewards, too. And there's another bonus. When you use all five keys three days in a row, you get an extra treat, something you can have or do right away. No waiting.

Maybe your parents can make up a grab bag of small gifts like nail polish, temporary tattoos, and your favorite kind of gum. Maybe you'd like extra time on the computer. Or to be excused from your worst chore. Each time you fill in all five keys three days in a row, a bonus like this can be yours.

Write three ideas for bonus rewards.

PSSST! THESE BONUS REWARDS ARE IN ADDITION TO YOUR 30-POINT REWARDS!

So work hard. Earn neat things. Wave your habit good-bye.

CHAPTER NINE

How's It Going?

How are things going with your habit?

You may think that checking the length of your fingernails will tell you how you're doing. Or watching your hair grow. Or your skin heal. But actually, these things can be a bit misleading.

If your nails are long, your hair is full, or your skin is smooth, that's great. It means you are breaking free from your habit.

But if your nails are jagged, or you have a bald patch or skin that's red and sore, what does that mean? Does it mean your plan has failed?

Not necessarily. You might have left your nails alone for eight whole days, and then on the ninth day you went on a nibbling SPREE. And that one spree is going to make your nails look awful. But that one spree, whatever it was about, is not as important as the eight days that came before it.

That's why your focus should never be on how long your nails are, or how your skin or hair is doing. Pay attention instead to the fact that you're spending less and less time doing your habit. That's what will happen as you continue to use your keys.

But what if it doesn't happen that way? What if you're using your keys—you really are—and your habit is still locked in place?

The first thing to do is to make sure you're using your keys often enough, especially in your danger zones. Sometimes danger zones change. Watch out for this, and have your keys on hand, ready to use.

If that doesn't do the trick, you and your parents will want to check out three possibilities:

Is Your Habit Really a Habit?

It may be that your habit isn't a habit at all. It could be a tic. A tic is a sound you make or a motion you do repeatedly, without realizing you're doing it. Blinking your eyes quickly is a common tic. So is making a noise in your throat, or scrunching your shoulders. Licking your lips can be a tic. Humming, too. There are lots of different tics.

Tics are really common, and they often come and go on their own. If you aren't sure whether what you do is a tic or a habit, talk to your mom and dad about going to see your doctor, who will be able to help you sort this out.

Usually tics aren't treated at all. You just live with them until they go away, although it's helpful to learn what to say to people who ask why you're shrugging or humming or doing whatever it is you do during your tic.

Even though tics are common, they can be stressful for kids and parents. If your tics are severe, or if they cause problems for you or other people, your doctor can help you find a therapist to teach you about tics and how to manage them.

Are There Big Problems in Your Life?

Perhaps something especially stressful is happening in your life. If so, you might need a bit of extra help.

Maybe someone in your family is sick, or your friends aren't treating you well. Maybe you have to move, or you hear your parents fighting a lot. If something like this is going on, you might have feelings that are hard to manage on your own.

Find a caring adult, such as your parents, or a teacher or therapist. Talk about how you feel and make a plan for how to cope.

And if something in particular—like worry or anger or sadness—often gets in your way, these same adults can help you learn to handle your feelings differently. Without big problems getting in the way, your habit-busting keys will work much better.

Are You Tired?

It may be that you aren't getting enough sleep. Kids who are 9 to 11 years old need at least 10 hours of sleep every night. Kids ages 8 and under need even more. Lack of sleep affects people in all kinds of ways. It's stressful for your brain and your body, making you more likely to pick, pull, twirl, suck, or chew.

Try getting more sleep. Kids who are well rested have an easier time doing all sorts of things. Including getting rid of habits.

Staying Free

Once you have unlocked yourself from your habit, you will be free. Congratulations! But don't let go of your habit-busting keys. They are the secret to *staying* free.

Keep using your keys every day. You'll notice that it gets easier and easier. That's because anything you do repeatedly turns into a habit. So after you have used your keys for three or more weeks, they'll turn into habits, too—this time the helpful kind.

You might put an interesting stone in your pocket every day to rub while you're on the bus. That's a habit based on the fiddle key. Or maybe you smooth lotion on your hands and feet before bed. That's a wake-up key habit for your skin.

And if you get bored, look back at the ideas in this book to find new ways to use your keys. These keys are the answer to breaking free and staying free. Hang on to them!

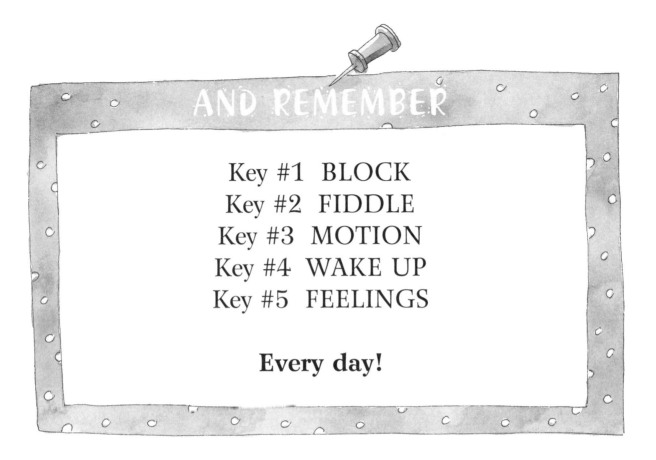

AND REMEMBER

Key #1 BLOCK
Key #2 FIDDLE
Key #3 MOTION
Key #4 WAKE UP
Key #5 FEELINGS

Every day!

Y O __ __ __ __

__ __ __ __ __!

It's going to feel so good!

Habit-Busting Keys

Keep track of your habit-busting strategies! Each time the book tells you to turn to this page, write in the name of the key you're learning about, and the activities that go along with it.

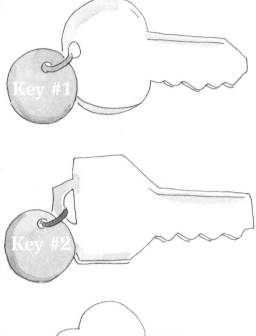

Block Plan

1. _____   4. _____
2. _____   5. _____
3. _____   6. _____

Fiddle Activities

1. _____   4. _____
2. _____   5. _____
3. _____   6. _____

Motion Ideas

1. _____
2. _____
3. _____

Wake-Up Ideas

1. _____
2. _____
3. _____

Tension Drainers

1. _____
2. _____
3. _____

Breaking Free

This chart will help you keep track of how often you're using your keys, and the rewards you are earning. Follow the directions on page 61 to watch yourself break free—and stay free!

Date	Keys Used	Points	Date	Keys Used	Points
	Block Fiddle Motion Wake-Up Feelings			Block Fiddle Motion Wake-Up Feelings	
	Block Fiddle Motion Wake-Up Feelings			Block Fiddle Motion Wake-Up Feelings	
	Block Fiddle Motion Wake-Up Feelings			Block Fiddle Motion Wake-Up Feelings	
	Block Fiddle Motion Wake-Up Feelings			Block Fiddle Motion Wake-Up Feelings	
	Block Fiddle Motion Wake-Up Feelings			Block Fiddle Motion Wake-Up Feelings	
	Block Fiddle Motion Wake-Up Feelings			Block Fiddle Motion Wake-Up Feelings	
	Block Fiddle Motion Wake-Up Feelings			Block Fiddle Motion Wake-Up Feelings	
	Block Fiddle Motion Wake-Up Feelings			Block Fiddle Motion Wake-Up Feelings	
	Block Fiddle Motion Wake-Up Feelings			Block Fiddle Motion Wake-Up Feelings	
	Block Fiddle Motion Wake-Up Feelings			Block Fiddle Motion Wake-Up Feelings	
	Block Fiddle Motion Wake-Up Feelings			Block Fiddle Motion Wake-Up Feelings	
	Block Fiddle Motion Wake-Up Feelings			Block Fiddle Motion Wake-Up Feelings	
	Block Fiddle Motion Wake-Up Feelings			Block Fiddle Motion Wake-Up Feelings	
	Block Fiddle Motion Wake-Up Feelings			Block Fiddle Motion Wake-Up Feelings	
	Block Fiddle Motion Wake-Up Feelings			Block Fiddle Motion Wake-Up Feelings	